Working in the U.K. A Foreigners Guide

Arthur Crandon LL.B (Hons), M.A.

Working in the UK

Copyright Arthur Crandon 2024

All rights reserved. No part of this book may be reproduced, stored in a retrieval system, or transmitted in any form or by any means—electronic, mechanical, photocopying, recording, or otherwise—without the prior written permission of the publisher, except for brief quotations in critical reviews or articles.

This is a work of fiction. Names, characters, places, and incidents are either the product of the author's imagination or used fictitiously. Any resemblance to actual persons, living or dead, events, or locales is entirely coincidental.

ISBN: 9798336506334

Cover design by Lynnie Ceniza
Interior design and formatting by Lynnie Ceniza
Published by Arthur Crandon Publishing
Visit our website: Arthurcrandon.co.uk

DISCLAIMER

The information provided in this book is for general informational purposes only. It does not constitute legal, financial, or professional advice. While every effort has been made to ensure accuracy, the author and publisher assume no responsibility for errors or omissions. Readers should consult with appropriate professionals for specific advice tailored to their individual circumstances.

First Edition: August 2024

Visit Arthurcrandon.co.uk for More Titles

Retirement to the Philippines
K1 Fiance visa to the U.S. – Fast Track
Secrets to buying Condos in the Philippines
Buying Land in the Philippines
Annulment in the Philippines
Breaking free from a bad marriage
Get a visit visa to America First time
Marriage in the Philippines
Get a visit visa to the United Kingdom
Ghosts, Spectres, and folklore in the Philippines
Retiring to Spain – a Comprehensive Guide
Spousal Visa to America
Spousal visa to the United Kingdom
Working in the UK

CONTENTS

1	Common work visas	1
2	Eligibility Requirements	7
3	Required Documents	13
4	Application Form	19
5	Fees and Biometrics	25
6	Supporting Documents	31
7	Interview and Result	37
8	Travel to the UK	43
9	Collect the BRP	49
10	Additional Tips	53

Forward

It is the goal of many people from other countries to come and work in the UK. We NEED workers from abroad in certain industries – the foreign office publishes list monthly of which workers will qualify for visa that month. Do not be tempted to go with fake agencies that say they will give you what you need to get in. They usually fail and you will lose a lot of money.
But if you are genuine, and are careful in your application, you should be fine. Very best wishes and good luck.

1 COMMON WORK VISAS

Detailed Guide on Common UK Work Visas

1. Skilled Worker Visa

- **Eligibility**: You must have a job offer from a UK employer who is a licensed sponsor. <u>The job must be on the list of eligible occupations and meet the minimum salary requirements</u>.

- **Requirements**:

  - Certificate of Sponsorship (CoS) from your employer.

  - Proof of English language proficiency.
  - Financial evidence to support

yourself.

- **Duration**: Up to 5 years, with the possibility to extend. <u>After 5 years, you may apply for indefinite leave to remain</u>.

2. Health and Care Worker Visa

- **<u>Eligibility</u>**: <u>For medical professionals with a job offer in the health or care sector from a licensed sponsor</u>.

- **Requirements**:

    o Certificate of Sponsorship (CoS) from your employer.

    o Proof of English language proficiency.

    o Financial evidence to support yourself.

- **<u>Benefits</u>**: <u>Reduced visa fees and exemption from the Immigration Health Surcharge</u>.

- **Duration**: Up to 5 years, with the possibility to extend. <u>After 5 years, you may apply for indefinite leave to remain</u>.

3. Global Talent Visa

- **Eligibility**: For leaders or potential leaders in academia, research, arts, and digital technology.

- **Requirements**:

  - Endorsement from a recognized UK body in your field.

  - Evidence of your exceptional talent or promise.

- **Benefits**: Flexibility to work in various roles without a specific job offer.

- **Duration**: Up to 5 years, with the possibility to extend. After 3 or 5 years, you may apply for indefinite leave to remain.

4. Graduate Visa

- **Eligibility**: For international students who have completed a degree in the UK.

- **Requirements**:

- Proof of graduation from a recognized UK institution.

- Valid student visa at the time of application.

- **Benefits**: Allows you to stay and work in the UK for up to 2 years (3 years for doctoral graduates) without a job offer.

- **Duration**: 2 years for bachelor's or master's graduates, 3 years for doctoral graduates.

5. Temporary Work Visa

- **Types**:
-
  - **Seasonal Worker Visa**: For temporary agricultural work.

  - **Charity Worker Visa**: For unpaid voluntary work with a registered charity.

  - **Creative Worker Visa**: For creative professionals such as actors, dancers, and musicians.

- **Requirements**:

  - Certificate of Sponsorship (CoS) from your employer.

  - Proof of English language proficiency (if applicable).

  - Financial evidence to support yourself.

- **Duration**: Varies by visa type, typically up to 12 months.

These details should help you understand the different types of work visas available for the UK and their specific requirements.

2 ELIGIBILTY REQUIREMENTS

Detailed Eligibility Requirements for UK Work Visas

1. Job Offer

- **Requirement**: Most work visas require a confirmed job offer from a UK employer who is a licensed sponsor.

- **Certificate of Sponsorship (CoS)**: Your employer must provide a Certificate of Sponsorship, which includes details about your job and confirms that they will sponsor your visa.

- **Eligible Occupations**: The job must be on the list of eligible occupations, which ensures it meets the skill level required for the visa.

2. English Language Proficiency

Requirement: You must prove your ability to speak, read, write, and understand English.

- **Accepted Tests**: Approved English language tests include IELTS, TOEFL, and others recognized by UK Visas and Immigration (UKVI).

- **Academic Qualifications**: If you have a degree taught in English, you can use this as proof. The degree must be equivalent to a UK bachelor's degree or higher and verified by Ecctis (formerly UK NARIC)

- **Exemptions**: Citizens of majority English-speaking countries and those with certain academic qualifications may be exempt from this requirement.

3. Financial Requirements

- **Requirement**: You must have enough money to support yourself without relying on public funds.

- **Maintenance Funds**: You need to show that you have a certain amount of money in your bank account for a specified period before applying. The exact amount varies depending on the visa type and your circumstances.

- **Employer Support**: In some cases, your employer can certify that they will cover your maintenance costs, which can help meet this requirement.

4. Qualifications and Experience

- **Requirement**: Depending on the visa, you may need relevant qualifications or work experience.

- **Skilled Worker Visa**: Requires a job that meets the skill level of RQF Level 3 (equivalent to A-level) or above.

- **Health and Care Worker Visa**: Requires qualifications and experience relevant to the healthcare sector.

- **Global Talent Visa**: Requires evidence of exceptional talent or promise in your field, such as awards, publications, or endorsements from recognized bodies.

Additional Considerations

- **Health and Character Requirements**: You may need to provide a tuberculosis (TB) test certificate if you are from a country where TB testing is required. Additionally, you must not have any criminal convictions that would make you ineligible for a visa.

- **Age Requirement**: Some visas, such as the Youth Mobility Scheme visa, have age restrictions. Ensure you meet the age criteria for the specific visa you are applying for.

These detailed eligibility requirements should help you understand what is needed to

apply for a UK work visa.

3 REQUIRED DOCUMENTS

Detailed Guide on Required Documents for UK Work Visas

1. Valid Passport

- **Requirement**: A current passport or travel document that confirms your identity and nationality.

- **Details**: Ensure your passport is valid for the duration of your stay in the UK and has at least one blank page for the visa vignette.

2. Job Offer

- **Certificate of Sponsorship (CoS)**:

  - **Requirement**: A unique reference number provided by your UK employer, who must be a licensed sponsor.

  - **Details**: The CoS includes information about your job, such as job title, salary, and occupation code. Your employer will provide this document.

3. Proof of English Proficiency

- **Accepted Tests**:

  - **Requirement**: Test results from approved English language tests like IELTS, TOEFL, or others recognized by UK Visas and Immigration (UKVI).

  - **Details**: The test must assess your ability to speak, read, write, and understand English.

- **Academic Qualifications**:

  - **Requirement**: If you have a degree taught in English, you can use this as proof.

  - **Details**: The degree must be equivalent to a UK bachelor's degree or higher and verified by Ecctis (formerly UK NARIC).

4. Financial Evidence

- **Maintenance Funds**:

  - **Requirement**: Proof that you have enough money to support yourself without relying on public funds.

  - **Details**: Bank statements showing a certain amount of money held for a specified period before applying. The exact amount varies depending on the visa type.

- **Employer Support**:

  - **Requirement**: In some cases, your employer can certify that they will cover your maintenance costs.

- o **Details**: This can help meet the financial requirement if your employer provides a letter confirming their support.

5. Qualifications

- **Academic Certificates**:

  - o **Requirement**: Certificates or transcripts of your academic qualifications.

  - o **Details**: These documents should demonstrate that you meet the educational requirements for your job. If your qualifications are from outside the UK, you may need to get them verified by Ecctis.

Additional Documents

- **Tuberculosis (TB) Test Results**:

  - o **Requirement**: If you are from a country where TB testing is required, provide a TB test certificate from an approved clinic.

- **Criminal Record Certificate**:

    o **Requirement**: If you are applying for certain jobs, such as in healthcare or education, you may need to provide a criminal record certificate.

- **Proof of Relationship**:

    o **Requirement**: If your partner or children are applying with you, provide documents proving your relationship, such as marriage or birth certificates.

These detailed requirements should help you gather all the necessary documents for your UK work visa application.

4 APPLICATION FORM

Completing the Application Form for a UK Work Visa

1. Online Application

- **Website**: Most visa applications are completed online through the UK Visas and Immigration (UKVI) website.

- **Account Creation**: You will need to create an account on the UKVI website to start your application.

- **Application Form**: Select the appropriate visa type and complete the online application form. The form will guide you through various sections, including personal details, employment information, and travel history.

2. Specific Forms

- **Skilled Worker Visa Application Form**: If you are applying for a Skilled Worker visa, you will need to complete the specific form for this visa type.

- **Other Visa Types**: Depending on your circumstances, you may need different forms, such as the Health and Care Worker visa form, Global Talent visa form, or Temporary Work visa form.

Steps to Complete the Application Form

1. **Personal Information**: Provide your full name, date of birth, nationality, and contact details.

2. **Passport Details**: Enter your passport number, issue date, and expiry date.

3. **Employment Information**: Include details about your job offer, such as the job title, salary, and Certificate of Sponsorship (CoS) reference number provided by your UK employer.

4. **Travel History**: List your travel history for the past 10 years, including countries visited and dates of travel.

5. **English Language Proficiency**: Indicate how you meet the English language requirement, whether through an approved test or academic qualification.

6. **Financial Evidence**: Provide details of your financial situation, including bank statements or proof of savings to show you can support yourself.

7. **Health Information**: If required, provide details of any tuberculosis (TB) test results or other medical information.

8. **Additional Information**: Answer any additional questions relevant to your visa type, such as criminal record checks or family details.

Paying the Application Fee

- **Visa Fee**: The fee varies depending on the visa type and duration of stay. Payment is usually made online during the application process.

- **Immigration Health Surcharge (IHS)**: You may also need to pay the IHS, which gives you access to the UK's National Health Service (NHS) during your stay.

Submitting the Application

- **Review**: Carefully review all the information entered in the application form to ensure accuracy.

- **Submit**: Once you are satisfied with the information, submit the application online.

- **Confirmation**: You will receive a confirmation email with details of your application and next steps.

Next Steps

- **Biometric Appointment**: You may need to book an appointment at a visa application center to provide biometric information (fingerprints and a photo).

- **Supporting Documents**: Upload or mail the required supporting documents as specified in the application instructions.

- **Track Application**: Use the reference number provided to track the status of your application online.

These detailed steps should help you complete the application form for your UK work visa

5 FEES AND BIOMETRIC INFORMATION

Pay the Application Fee

Visa Application Fees

- **Skilled Worker Visa:**

  - Up to 3 years: £719 if applying from outside the UK; £827 if applying from inside the UK.

  - More than 3 years: £1,420 if applying from outside the UK; £1,636 if applying from inside the UK.

- **Health and Care Worker Visa:**

  - Up to 3 years: £247.

  - More than 3 years: £479

- **Global Talent Visa:**

  - Main applicant: £608.

  - Dependents: £608 each.

- **Graduate Visa: £715**

- **Temporary Work Visa:**

  - Seasonal Worker: £259.

  - Charity Worker: £259.

  - Creative Worker: £259.

Immigration Health Surcharge (IHS)

- Cost: £624 per year for most applicants

- Purpose: Provides access to the UK's National Health Service (NHS) during your stay.

Payment Process

- Online Payment: Fees are usually paid online during the application process. You will be prompted to enter your payment details after completing the application form.

- Confirmation: After payment, you will receive a confirmation email with details of your payment and next steps

6. Provide Biometric Information

What is Biometric Information?

- Fingerprints: Scanned electronically.

- Digital Photograph: A photo of your face taken at the visa application center.

Why is it Required?

Biometric information is used to:

- Verify your identity.

- Issue a Biometric Residence Permit (BRP), which serves as proof of your right to stay in the UK.

Where to Provide Biometric Information

- Outside the UK: You will need to visit a visa application center in your country of residence.

- Inside the UK: You can provide biometric information at a UK Visa and Citizenship Application Services (UKVCAS) service point or a Service and Support Centre (SSC)

Steps to Provide Biometric Information

1. Book an Appointment: After submitting your online application, you will be prompted to book an appointment at a visa application center.

2. Attend the Appointment: Bring your passport and appointment confirmation. The process typically takes less than 5 minutes.

3. Fingerprints: Place your fingers on a glass screen to be scanned. This is a clean and quick process.

4. Digital Photograph: A digital photo of your face will be taken. You do not need to remove head coverings worn for religious or medical reasons.

5. Children: Children under 16 must be accompanied by a parent or guardian. Children under 5 do not need to provide fingerprints.

These details should help you understand the process of paying the application fee and providing biometric information for your UK work visa.

6 DOCUMENTS

Submitting Supporting Documents for a UK Work Visa

1. Preparing Your Documents

- **Originals and Copies**: Always provide original documents unless specifically stated otherwise by UK Visas and Immigration (UKVI). Make clear, legible copies of all documents.

- **Translations**: If any documents are not in English or Welsh, they must be accompanied by a full translation that can be independently verified by the Home Office. Each translation must include:

- Confirmation from the translator that it is an accurate translation of the original document.

- The date of translation.

- The translator's full name and signature.

- The translator's contact details.

2. Organizing Your Documents

- **Order of Documents**: Arrange your documents in the order listed in the visa application guidelines. This typically includes:

  - Passport and travel documents.

  - Certificate of Sponsorship (CoS).

  - Proof of English language proficiency.

o   Financial evidence.

o   Academic qualifications.

o   Additional documents specific to your visa type.

- **Labelling and Securing**: Label each document clearly and securely fasten them together. Use paper clips or folders to keep related documents together.

3. Uploading Documents Online

- **Self-Upload Service**: If you use the 'UK Immigration: ID Check' app to scan your identity document, you can use the self-upload service when you apply.

- **Scanning and Photos**: You can either scan your documents or take photos of them. Ensure the full document is visible and in focus. Save the images as PNG, JPG, or JPEG files.

- **Uploading Process**:

  o Log in to your UKVI account.

  o Follow the instructions to upload each document. You may need to upload the same document more than once if it is required in multiple sections.

  o Give each file a descriptive name, such as 'passport' or 'bank statement 2024'

4. Mailing Documents

- **When to Mail**: If you cannot use the self-upload service, you may need to mail your documents to the appropriate address provided by UKVI.

- **Mailing Instructions**:

  o Use a secure and trackable mailing service.

  o Include a cover letter listing all the documents you are sending.

o Ensure all documents are securely packaged to prevent damage during transit.

5. Additional Tips

- **Review Before Submission**: Double-check all documents for accuracy and completeness before submission. Ensure all required documents are included.

- **Keep Copies**: Keep copies of all documents for your records. This can be helpful if any issues arise during the application process.

- **Track Your Application**: Use the reference number provided to track the status of your application online.

These detailed steps should help you successfully submit your supporting documents for your UK work visa application.

7 INTERVIEW AND RESULT

7. Attend an Interview (if required)

When an Interview is Required

- **Notification**: You will be informed if an interview is required as part of your visa application process. This can happen if additional information is needed or if there are any concerns about your application.

- **Types of Interviews**: Interviews can be conducted face-to-face at a visa application center or electronically via video call.

Preparing for the Interview

- **Documents to Bring**: Bring all relevant documents, including your passport, application form, and any supporting documents you submitted.

- **Common Questions**: Be prepared to answer questions about:

  - Your job offer and employer.

  - Your qualifications and work experience.

  - Your financial situation and how you plan to support yourself in the UK.

  - Your travel history and reasons for moving to the UK.

- **Practice**: Practice answering potential questions confidently and clearly. It can be helpful to review your application and supporting documents beforehand.

During the Interview

- **Verification**: The interviewer will verify your identity and the information provided in your application.

- **Questions**: Answer all questions honestly and provide any additional information requested. The interviewer may take notes during the interview.

- **Duration**: Interviews typically last between 15 to 30 minutes, but this can vary depending on the complexity of your case.

8. Wait for a Decision

Processing Times

- **Outside the UK**: The standard processing time for work visa applications made from outside the UK is usually **3 weeks**.

- **Inside the UK**: If applying from within the UK, the processing time is typically **8 weeks**.

- **Extended Processing**: Processing times may be longer if additional checks are needed, such as verifying documents or conducting an interview.

Tracking Your Application

- **Online Tracking**: You can track the status of your application online through the UK Visas and Immigration (UKVI) website. You will need your application reference number to check the status.

- **Notifications**: You will receive email updates regarding the progress of your application. Once a decision is made, you will be notified by email or letter.

Receiving the Decision

- **Decision Letter**: You will receive a letter or email informing you of the decision on your visa application. This will include instructions on the next steps.

- **Vignette**: If your application is approved, you will receive a vignette (sticker) in your passport. This vignette allows you to travel to and enter the UK.

- **Biometric Residence Permit (BRP)**: Once in the UK, you will need to collect your BRP. The BRP is a physical card that confirms your identity and immigration status.

Collecting the BRP

- **Collection Point**: The decision letter will specify where to collect the BRP, usually from a designated Post Office branch or your sponsor's address if chosen during the application.

- **Timeframe**: You must collect your BRP within 10 days of arriving in the UK or before the vignette expires, whichever is later.

- **Required Documents**: To collect the BRP, bring your passport with the vignette and the decision letter.

These details should help you understand the process of attending an interview (if required) and waiting for a decision on your UK work visa application.

8 TRAVEL TO THE UK

Preparing for Travel

- **Documents to Carry**: Ensure you have all relevant documents, including:

  - **Passport**: Your passport with the visa vignette.

  - **Decision Letter**: The letter from UK Visas and Immigration (UKVI) confirming your visa approval.

  - **Supporting Documents**: Copies of your visa application and supporting documents, such as proof of relationship, financial evidence, and accommodation details.

o **Travel Itinerary**: Details of your flight and accommodation bookings.

o **Contact Information**: Contact details of your UK sponsor or employer.

Before Departure

- **Check Travel Restrictions**: Verify any travel restrictions or requirements due to health or security concerns.

- **Health Insurance**: Consider obtaining travel health insurance to cover any medical expenses during your journey.

- **Currency**: Ensure you have some British pounds (GBP) for immediate expenses upon arrival.

At the Airport

- **Check-in**: Arrive at the airport early to allow sufficient time for check-in and security checks.

- **Security Screening**: Be prepared for security screening, including removing electronic devices and liquids from your carry-on luggage.

During the Flight

- **In-Flight Documents**: Keep your passport, visa vignette, and decision letter accessible during the flight.

- **Arrival Card**: Some airlines may provide an arrival card to fill out before landing. This card will be collected by UK border control upon arrival.

Upon Arrival in the UK

- **Border Control**: Present your passport with the visa vignette to the border control officer. Be prepared to answer questions about the purpose of your visit and provide any requested documents.
- **Biometric Residence Permit (BRP)**: If you

received a vignette, you must collect your BRP within 10 days of arriving in the UK or before the vignette expires, whichever is later.

Collecting the BRP

- **Collection Point**: The decision letter will specify where to collect the BRP, usually from a designated Post Office branch or your sponsor's address if chosen during the application.

- **Required Documents**: To collect the BRP, bring your passport with the vignette and the decision letter.

Settling In

- **Accommodation**: Ensure your accommodation is ready and accessible upon arrival.

- **Local Transportation**: Familiarize yourself with local transportation options to reach your accommodation from the airport.

- **Emergency Contacts**: Keep a list of emergency contacts, including your sponsor or employer, local authorities, and medical services.

These detailed steps should help you prepare for your travel to the UK and ensure a smooth entry process.

9 COLLECT THE BRP

Collect the Biometric Residence Permit (BRP)

What is a BRP?

- **Biometric Residence Permit (BRP)**: A BRP is a card that contains your biometric information (fingerprints and photo) and details about your immigration status. It serves as proof of your right to stay, work, or study in the UK.

Collection Process

- **Timeframe**: You must collect your BRP within 10 days of arriving in the UK or before the vignette sticker in your passport expires, whichever is later.

- **Collection Point**: The decision letter will specify where to collect your BRP, usually from a designated Post Office branch or your sponsor's address if chosen during the application.

Steps to Collect the BRP

1. **Locate the Collection Point**: Check your decision letter for the specified Post Office branch or sponsor's address.

2. **Visit the Collection Point**: Go to the designated location within the specified timeframe.

3. **Present Documents**: Bring your passport with the visa vignette and the decision letter to the staff at the collection point.

4. **Receive the BRP**: The staff will verify your documents and hand over your BRP.

Additional Information

- **Collecting for a Child**: If you are collecting a BRP for a child, you must be nominated to do so, even if you are the child's parent. The Home Office will inform you within 5 working days if you are approved to collect the child's BRP.

- **Changing Collection Location**: If you need to collect your BRP from a different Post Office branch, you can arrange this at the desired branch and pay a fee. Ensure the branch offers a 'BRP collection service'.

- **Leaving and Re-entering the UK**: If you need to leave and re-enter the UK before collecting your BRP, you must apply for a 'replacement BRP visa' to re-enter the UK.

Important Considerations

- **Failure to Collect**: If you do not collect your BRP within the specified timeframe, you may face penalties or issues with your immigration status.

- **Proof of Status**: The BRP is essential for proving your right to stay, work, or study in the UK. Keep it safe and carry it with you when needed.

These details should help you understand the process of collecting your BRP after arriving in the UK.

10 ADDITIONAL TIPS

Additional Tips for Legally Working in the UK

Right to Work Check

- **Purpose**: The right to work check ensures that you are legally allowed to work in the UK. Employers are required by law to conduct this check before you start your job.

- **Process**:

    o **Document Verification**: Your employer will ask to see your original documents, such as your passport and visa. They will check the validity of these documents and make copies for their records.

- ○ **Online Right to Work Check**: If you have a Biometric Residence Permit (BRP), you can use the online right to work checking service. You will need to provide your employer with a share code and your date of birth so they can verify your status online.

- **Frequency**: The check is usually done once before you start your job. However, if your visa has an expiry date, your employer may need to conduct follow-up checks to ensure you continue to have the right to work.

Stay Informed

- **Immigration Laws and Policies**: Immigration laws and policies can change, affecting your visa status and work rights. Staying informed helps you remain compliant and avoid any legal issues.

- **Resources**:

- **GOV.UK**: Regularly check the GOV.UK website for updates on immigration laws and policies.

- **Legal Advice**: Consider seeking advice from immigration lawyers or consultants who can provide personalized guidance based on your situation.

- **Employer Support**: Your employer's HR department may also provide updates and support regarding changes in immigration policies.

Additional Considerations

- **Workplace Rights**: Familiarize yourself with your rights as an employee in the UK, including working hours, minimum wage, and health and safety regulations.

- **Cultural Adaptation**: Adjusting to the UK work culture can enhance your experience. Understanding workplace etiquette, communication styles, and social norms can help you integrate smoothly.
- **Networking**: Building a professional

network can open up opportunities and provide support. Attend industry events, join professional associations, and connect with colleagues and peers.

- **Professional Development**: Take advantage of training and development opportunities offered by your employer or external organizations to enhance your skills and career prospects.

These additional tips should help you navigate the process of legally working in the UK and ensure a smooth transition.

Visit Arthurcrandon.co.uk for More Titles

Retirement to the Philippines
K1 Fiance visa to the U.S. – Fast Track
Secrets to buying Condos in the Philippines
Buying Land in the Philippines
Annulment in the Philippines
Breaking free from a bad marriage
Get a visit visa to America First time
Marriage in the Philippines
Get a visit visa to the United Kingdom
Ghosts, Spectres, and folklore in the Philippines
Retiring to Spain – a Comprehensive Guide
Spousal Visa to America
Spousal visa to the United Kingdom
Working in the UK.

ABOUT THE AUTHOR

Arthur Crandon is a retired lawyer and a prolific writer. Hi is British and grew up in a rural community in Somerset. He has lived in England, Wales, Hong Kong and the Philippines and now spends most of his time in the Philippines with his Visayan wife and their son.

He loves to hear from anyone who has anything to do with the Philippines – you can email him anytime on:

ac@arthurcrandon.co.uk

www.ingramcontent.com/pod-product-compliance
Lightning Source LLC
Chambersburg PA
CBHW070216230526
45471CB00002B/963